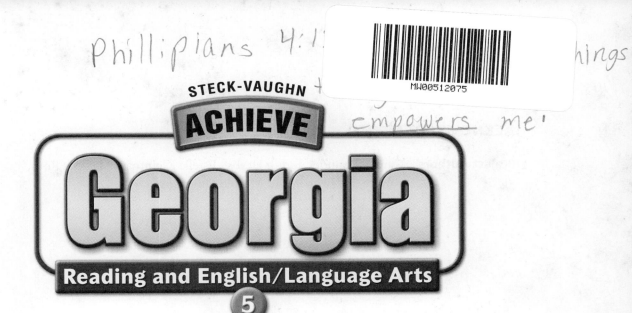

STECK-VAUGHN
ACHIEVE

Georgia
Reading and English/Language Arts
5

* Goal 20 correct answers
to make
800

CRCT = Criterion
Refrence
Competency   Know   Strategies
Test

Authors purpose   1. Antonymn   1. Calm down
                                 2. Synonymn   2. Read questions first
1. To persuade   3. Main idea   3. Reread passage as much
2. To inform   4. Compound word   as you need
3. To entertain   4. Look back for answers

Harcourt Achieve
Rigby · Steck-Vaughn

www.HarcourtAchieve.com
1.800.531.5015

ACKNOWLEDGMENTS

Project Authors Carol Alexander, Judith Herbst, Estelle Kleinman, Marlene Roth, Sandra Shichtman, and Marren Simmons

The Georgia Department of Education, the publisher of the Georgia Criterion-Referenced Competency Tests, has neither endorsed nor authorized this test-preparation book.

ISBN 0-7398-9487-0

© 2005 Harcourt Achieve Inc.

1 2 3 4 5 6 7 8 9 10 082 11 10 09 08 07 06 05 04

Achieve Georgia
Contents

Georgia Reading and English/Language Arts Standards

Achieve Georgia will help you get ready for a test based on the standards set up by the state of Georgia. Standards are goals that have been developed to make sure that you have all the skills necessary to be successful in school.

Reading for Vocabulary Improvement

Can you use clues to figure out the meanings of words? Do you know how to use context clues to figure out the meanings of words you do not know? Can you recognize a compound word?

Reading for Locating and Recalling Information

Do you know how to follow directions? Can you figure out the main idea of a passage?

Can you find details that support the main idea? Do you know what a cause is? Do you know what an effect is?

Reading for Meaning

Do you know the difference between a story and a poem? Can you recognize fiction and nonfiction writing? Can you tell what a story is about? Do you know how to describe the characters in a story? Do you know how to tell what will happen next in a story?

Sentence Construction and Revision

Do you know the rules for using language correctly when you write? Can you write a good sentence? Can you recognize errors in writing? Do you know how to fix these errors?

Research Process

Do you know the correct alphabetical order of words? Do you know how to find things in different kinds of books? Can you put your ideas together in an organized way?

To the Student

This book will help you prepare for a test based on the Criterion-Referenced Competency Test (CRCT) in Reading and English/Language Arts. The first part of the book, Modeled Instruction, will give you practice with the different kinds of questions you will see on the real test. The Modeled Instruction will also give you tips for answering each question.

The second part of the book, the Practice Test, is similar to the CRCT. Taking the Practice Test will help you know what the actual CRCT is like.

The CRCT includes questions about Reading and English/Language Arts. The CRCT asks you to answer questions about what you have read.

The questions about Reading will have you read a passage. Then you will answer the questions about the passage. You may be asked to decide about vocabulary, or to recall information from the passage, or to explain what you have read.

The questions about English/Language Arts will ask you to choose the best answer for questions about using language. You may find errors in sentences or show that you know how to find information in different kinds of books or sources.

Multiple Choice Items

After each multiple-choice item are four answer choices. In Modeled Instruction, circle the letter next to the answer. For the Practice Test, you will need to fill in the circle of each correct answer on the answer sheet.

Modeled Instruction
Reading

Reading has 24 questions and is divided into Section 1 and Section 2. Read each passage. For each question, choose the one best answer and circle the letter next to the answer.

This story is about Marcus, who had to choose something important to him for a time capsule at school. To find out what Marcus chose and why, read the passage and answer the questions that follow.

The Thing About Marcus

Marcus and his class were making a time capsule. Every student was supposed to put in an object, and each object was supposed to stand for something special about the student that chose it. After twenty years, the capsule would be opened and the objects removed. It would be interesting to see if what was important to a student in the fifth grade would still be important twenty years later.

Marcus was having trouble deciding on a special thing. If he put something special in the time capsule, he would have to live without it for twenty years.

"You could put in that model airplane you built," suggested his friend Mai.

"I won't give up my airplane," Marcus replied. "It reminds me that I want to be a pilot when I grow up!"

"Maybe that's just why you should put it in," she replied.

Marcus didn't want to think about giving up his plane. He thought instead of what else he could give up. He thought about a program from the school play when he had played a mighty oak tree, but he realized that the program wasn't important enough. Then he thought of his favorite book, but he knew it would be due back at the library soon. After school that day his mother saw that he could use some help.

"Maybe you're thinking about the wrong things, Marcus," she said. "Instead of thinking about which thing, maybe you should think about what a 'thing' really is."

"A thing is a thing—that's all, Mom," Marcus said.

"That's right, Marcus. Now think about that for a while," his mother said.

Marcus thought about what Mai and his mother had said. Suddenly, a <u>clear</u> idea popped into his mind. He knew what to do. He wrapped up his favorite model airplane to take to school and attached a short, simple note:

"Marcus's airplane," it read, "is very important to him, but it is just a toy and not the same as a dream of being a pilot. The dream stays with him no matter what because it is the most important thing."

**PLEASE GO ON TO
THE NEXT PAGE.** ⮞

1. Why did Marcus change his mind and select his model airplane for the time capsule?

   A. Mai said that he should be a pilot.

   B. He decided he can write a note and explain why he chose it.

   C. His mother said he is thinking about the wrong things.

   D. He realized he did not need his toy to remind him of his dream.

   Tip: The plot of a story is made up of each action or event. Look at the events that happen before and after Marcus makes his decision. They will tell you why Marcus acted as he did.

   "Suddenly, a _clear_ idea popped into his mind."

2. Which phrase is a synonym for _clear_?

   A. without worry

   B. without thought

   C. without confusion

   D. without fear

   Tip: Many words have more than one meaning. Sometimes sentences around the word contain clues to the word's meaning. Look in the story at the sentence that follows the word _clear_. Ask yourself what that sentence means.

3. This passage is an example of

   A. a play.

   B. a story.

   C. a poem.

   D. a letter.

   Tip: Authors decide what form of writing they will use to communicate their ideas. A play is dialogue between characters. Fiction is a story based on make-believe events and characters. A poem uses rhyme and rhythm. A letter has an inside address, a greeting, and a closing. Look back over the passage to decide what kind of writing the author has chosen.

4. What is a "time capsule" as mentioned in the passage?

   A. a model airplane

   B. a box of library books

   C. a container for special objects

   D. a program from a school play

   Tip: Writers include details to support their main ideas and to make passages interesting. In this passage, the time capsule is an important detail. To locate its meaning, skim the first paragraph of the passage and look for the term _time capsule_, and read to see how it is explained.

Georgia Reading Standards

1. **5.53:** Responds appropriately to questions about author's purpose, techniques, character development and plot structures.
2. **5.23:** Demonstrates an understanding of semantic relationships by using context clues, word meanings, and prior knowledge in reading.
3. **5.20:** Reads for a variety of purposes in different kinds of texts.
4. **5.27:** Recognized EXPLICIT main ideas, details, sequence of events and cause-effect relationships in fiction and nonfiction.

PLEASE GO ON TO THE NEXT PAGE.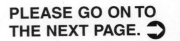

This passage shows some surprising results from droughts. To find out the effects of drought on birds in the Florida Everglades, read the passage and answer the questions that follow.

Good News About Droughts

Usually, people think of long periods without rain as being bad for the environment. Scientists in Florida have recently discovered some good news about droughts. In years following droughts, the number of birds nesting in the Everglades is greater than normal. But what causes the number of birds nesting to be higher? That very question puzzled Peter Frederick, an expert on birds that wade in the waters of Florida.

Several kinds of birds—white ibis, wood storks, snowy egrets, and tricolor herons—spend their entire lives around water. They hunt for fish to eat, and they build their nests in the tall grasses beside the water. After a long drought in the 1990s, Peter Frederick expected that the population of these wading birds would decrease. Instead, to his surprise, the bird population boomed.

Frederick began looking into the records that had been kept about birds and droughts. He discovered that eight droughts had occurred between 1931 and 1998. He found that after seven out of the eight droughts, the birds began multiplying at a fast rate. For example, instead of the 10,000 nesting birds that usually were around the waters, as many as 150,000 birds were nesting after a drought.

Frederick talked to his friend John Ogden, another scientist. Together they decided that two things caused the bird population to increase.

Their first explanation has to do with fire. During droughts, wildfires often occur. These fires release ash and other materials into the environment. After droughts end, these materials are sucked up by plants during floods. Birds feed on these plants. The helpful qualities of these materials help birds stay healthy. This increases the chances that the birds and their chicks survive.

Their second explanation has to do with fish. During droughts, the number of fish decreases. For example, most big fish and the little fish they eat die. However, the little fish have a faster life cycle. There are many more little fish in the years after a drought, and there are not as many big fish to eat them. Suddenly there are thousands of little fish. The birds then feed on these fish. The amount of fish available helps birds stay healthy. This increases the chances that the birds and their chicks survive as well.

Scientists are still working to prove their explanations. If they're right, people may just have a good reason to change the way they think about droughts.

PLEASE GO ON TO THE NEXT PAGE. ➜

5. How does ash from fire help the birds?

   A. It makes the sky cloudy.

   B. It gives them a place to live.

   C. It helps the plants they eat.

   D. It gives them warmth in winter.

> ⑨ **Tip:** Causes and effects are often arranged in order, even when the writer does not use clue words. Reread the sentences that talk about ash and plants to find the connection between the ash and the birds.

6. A word that has a meaning similar to the word *right* in this passage is

   A. good.

   B. correct.

   C. fair.

   D. legal.

> ⑨ **Tip:** A word that means the same or nearly the same as another word is called a synonym. Reread the last two sentences of the final paragraph. Think about how the word *right* is used in the last paragraph.

7. The author most likely wrote this passage to

   A. tell the history of birds living in the Everglades.

   B. persuade people that droughts are good for plants and birds.

   C. describe the work of two leading scientists in Florida.

   D. explain the possible reasons for increased number of birds after droughts.

> ⑨ **Tip:** Authors write for many purposes, such as to persuade, to entertain, and to inform. Informational passages usually explain one main topic. Think about what kind of information the author tells you.

8. What will most likely happen in the Everglades after the next drought?

   A. The number of birds will increase.

   B. The number of fires will decrease.

   C. New types of birds will come to live there.

   D. Scientists will stop studying the birds after droughts.

> ⑨ **Tip:** Often you can make a prediction by reviewing the passage. The first paragraph states what usually happens in the Everglades after a drought. Based on that, you can guess what will probably happen after another drought.

Georgia Reading Standards
5. **5.28:** Recognizes IMPLICIT main ideas, details, sequence of events, and cause-effect relationships in fiction and nonfiction.
6. **5.37:** Uses knowledge of synonyms, antonyms, and homophones when reading.
7. **5.29:** Identifies story development, author's purpose, and point of view.
8. **5.31:** Draws conclusions, makes predictions, compares/contrasts, and makes generalizations.

PLEASE GO ON TO THE NEXT PAGE. ➔

Modeled Instruction • 7

James Oglethorpe is an important figure in the history of Georgia. To learn more about the founder of the colony of Georgia, read this passage and answer the questions that follow.

The Caring Colonist

James Edward Oglethorpe was born in London, England, in 1696. He lived a great adventure, beginning a new colony in the New World.

In the 1720s, Oglethorpe studied England's prisons. People in prisons at that time lived in very bad conditions. They could be sent to jail for owing someone money. In fact, one of Oglethorpe's good friends died in prison after getting smallpox. That event changed Oglethorpe's life.

Oglethorpe had an idea for a colony where poor people from England could make a new start. He would name it after King George II, the king of England. He and several of his friends, who were also concerned about prisons in England, got a charter for all the land between the Altamaha and Savannah Rivers. None of the charter holders could make money from the colony. From the first, the colony was to help poor people.

It took years to make the plans for the colony. Finally, in 1733 Oglethorpe brought the first settlers to the New World. He brought 114 men, women, and children. The settlers were carpenters, tailors, bakers, farmers, merchants, and others with skills that could help the new colony. However, not one of the people selected to come to Georgia had been in prison because of owing money.

They first landed in South Carolina. Oglethorpe and a group of men then went south to look at the land that their charter had given them. They liked what they saw. They put ashore at the present-day Savannah and met two traders who helped them. Then Oglethorpe returned to South Carolina and brought the colonists to the land they were to settle.

They began to build the city of Savannah. Building a new city is hard work. But the colonists trusted Oglethorpe. He encouraged the colonists to plant crops and build the city themselves. They would not force anyone to help them.

Oglethorpe was a leader who also was a doctor and judge to the families in his colony. He liked things to run smoothly, and he liked people to be orderly. He wanted to protect the people in his colony.

Oglethorpe respected all the colonists. It did not matter if they had been rich or poor before they came to the New World. It costs a great deal of money to build a new town. To help support the colony, Oglethorpe went back to England several times and spent his own money to help the settlers survive. In 1743 he returned to England and began a career in government. The colonists were sad to see him leave.

PLEASE GO ON TO THE NEXT PAGE. ➲

9. Why did Oglethorpe want to create a colony in the New World?

A. He felt like having an adventure.

B. He wanted to give poor people a new start.

C. He was tired of living in England.

D. He dreamed of becoming governor of Georgia.

🌀 **Tip:** Often important ideas are supported by details in a passage. Look for the event or idea that led to Oglethorpe's desire to create a colony.

10. The author's purpose in writing this passage is to

A. argue that prisons in England should be changed.

B. suggest that people should be interested in Georgia history.

C. tell about the man who began the Georgia colony.

D. explain the life of Native Americans in Georgia.

🌀 **Tip:** An author may write to describe or explain something, to persuade, or to entertain readers. Authors use facts to explain and opinions to persuade. Ask yourself what kind of factual information the author gives about James Oglethorpe and his work in founding Georgia.

11. In this passage, the word *encouraged* means

A. asked.

B. taught.

C. ordered.

D. inspired.

🌀 **Tip:** Often you can figure out an unknown word by looking for clues in the sentences around it. Reread the sentences around the word *encouraged* and think about what kind of leader Oglethorpe was for the colonists.

12. What is Oglethorpe's "great adventure" mentioned in the passage?

A. what Oglethorpe did

B. when Oglethorpe lived

C. who Oglethorpe helped

D. when Oglethorpe studied

🌀 **Tip:** Sometimes authors use terms to summarize actions that they explain in their passages. Skim through the passage and take note of Oglethorpe's activities. Then decide how the term *great adventure* summarizes Oglethorpe's experience in Georgia.

This page may not be reproduced without permission of Harcourt Achieve.

Georgia Reading Standards
9. 5.27: Recognizes EXPLICIT main idea, details, sequence of events, and cause-effect relationships in fiction and nonfiction.
10. 5.29: Identifies story development, author's purpose, and point of view.
11. 5.37: Uses knowledge of synonyms, antonyms, and homophones when reading.
12. 5.27: Recognizes EXPLICIT main idea, details, sequence of events, and cause-effect relationships in fiction and nonfiction.

STOP!

Modeled Instruction
Reading

The Ocoee River has interesting uses for its water flow. To find out how the Ocoee River generates electricity for homes and businesses and creates excitement for kayaking, read the passage and answer the questions that follow.

Using the Ocoee River

During 1996 Atlanta hosted the Summer Olympics. One of the events held was whitewater kayaking. This event involves racing down a river's rapids. This fast-moving water makes the sport exciting but dangerous. The river used to host the event was the Ocoee River. But did you know that the Ocoee River does not normally have rapids?

A group called the Tennessee Valley Authority controls the flow of the river. Sometimes, the river is used to create electricity. When creating electricity, there is little water in the river. There's not even enough water for kayaking. Other times, the river is used for kayaking. This means that the Ocoee River needs a lot of water. So how is the water level controlled?

It all starts 28 miles upriver at Ocoee River Dam Number 3. To create electricity, the river's water is sent downstream. It travels through a tunnel that is 2.5 miles long. From the tunnel, it ends up at a power station. There, the water is used to create electricity. For kayaking, the water is sent upstream. It is then sent into the river. Adding this extra water to the river creates rapids. This water can then be used for kayaking. It takes the water about two hours to reach the river. This means that it must be released a few hours before a kayaking race.

The river wasn't just used for kayaking during the Olympics. When it isn't creating electricity, it is still used for kayaking and rafting. The group controlling the river has an important balance to maintain. It must make electricity for Georgia while still letting Georgians have fun on the water.

**PLEASE GO ON TO
THE NEXT PAGE.** ➜

13. In this passage, the word *rapids* means

A. deep water.

B. warm water.

C. bubbly water.

D. swift water.

> **Tip:** Often, clues to the meaning of a new word can be found in the passage. To find the meaning of the word *rapids*, read the next sentence and notice the word *fast-moving water*. Decide how these words might be related to *rapids*.

14. Which word has a suffix that means *the act of*?

A. downstream

B. dangerous

C. kayaking

D. hosted

> **Tip:** A suffix is an ending attached to a root word. Remember that compound words are formed by joining two shorter words together. The suffix *–ous* means *full of*. The suffix *–ing* can mean a *process or act of*. An *–ed* may be added to a verb to create the past tense. Decide which word has the correct suffix.

15. Which is an opinion?

A. During 1996 Atlanta hosted the Summer Olympics.

B. One of the events held was whitewater kayaking.

C. This fast-moving water makes the sport exciting but dangerous.

D. The river used to host the event was the Ocoee River.

> **Tip:** An opinion is a statement that expresses a person's ideas or feelings. People may agree or disagree with an opinion. A fact is a statement that can be proved. Think about which statement cannot be proved.

16. According to the passage, what happens to the river when electricity is created?

A. The water races downstream.

B. There is little water in the river.

C. The water gets pumped upstream.

D. The water takes two hours to create electricity.

> **Tip:** Sometimes authors include both causes and effects in their explanations of events. Reread the second and third paragraphs and notice the explanation of how electricity is created. Ask yourself what happens as a result of creating electricity.

This page may not be reproduced without permission of Harcourt Achieve.

Georgia Reading Standards
13. **5.23:** Demonstrates an understanding of semantic relationships by using context clues, word meanings, and prior knowledge in reading.
14. **5.36:** Uses knowledge of root words, prefixes, and suffixes in word recognition.
15. **5.56:** Distinguishes between fact and opinion.
16. **5.28:** Recognizes EXPLICIT main ideas, details, sequence of events and cause-effect relationships in fiction and nonfiction.

PLEASE GO ON TO THE NEXT PAGE. ➜

To learn how to make French toast, read the passage and answer the questions that follow.

French Toast

2 eggs

$\frac{1}{2}$ teaspoon vanilla

$\frac{1}{2}$ teaspoon cinnamon

$\frac{1}{8}$ cup milk

4 pieces of bread

$\frac{1}{2}$ cup of berries or maple syrup

Step 1. Break eggs into bowl. Be sure there are no pieces of eggshell in the bowl. Add vanilla, cinnamon, and milk. Mix with a fork until blended and smooth.

Step 2. Preheat a nonstick frying pan over medium heat. Ask an adult to help you with the stove and frying pan.

Step 3. Work with one slice of bread at a time. Dip each side of the bread into the mixture until lightly coated.

Step 4. Carefully place each slice of bread in the pan with a spatula (flat kitchen tool).

Step 5. Heat each side of bread for about three minutes, or until lightly browned. Use the spatula to turn the slices.

Step 6. Transfer the French toast to a plate. Cut the French toast into two or four triangles, using a table knife. Serve with berries or syrup.

PLEASE GO ON TO THE NEXT PAGE. ➲

17. Which step comes after dipping the bread in the mixture?

    A. mixing the ingredients

    B. cracking the eggs

    C. placing the pan on the stove

    D. placing bread in the pan

> **Tip:** Directions are usually listed in order from start to finish. Reread the directions, looking for the words *bread* and *dip*. Then read what comes after that direction.

"Be sure there are no pieces of eggshell in the bowl."

---

18. *Eggshell* is an example of a

    A. contraction.

    B. metaphor.

    C. compound word.

    D. possessive noun.

> **Tip:** Recognizing how different words are used will help you understand directions more clearly. A metaphor is a word picture. A compound word is a word made by joining two smaller words together. A possessive noun would have an *'s*. Then decide what kind of word *eggshell* is.

19. Which could you substitute for the fork in the recipe?

    A. a bowl

    B. a plate

    C. a spoon

    D. a frying pan

> **Tip:** Sometimes you can use different tools and still follow directions. Think about how the fork is being held and turned. Then choose the object that can be used in the same way.

20. The author's purpose in writing this passage is to

    A. convince readers to change their eating habits.

    B. tell readers an exciting story about cooking.

    C. persuade readers to learn to use spices.

    D. inform readers with specific directions.

> **Tip:** Authors usually make their purposes clear in the language they choose and the order in which they present the information. Notice that this passage lists ingredients and directions. Decide whether the author intended to persuade, entertain, or inform the readers.

Georgia Reading Standards
17. 5.18: Follows written directions.
18. 5.35: Recognizes and reads compound words, contractions, possessives, and words containing the suffixes "ing," "ed," "s," and "es."
19. 5.17: Classifies and categorizes words into sets and groups with common characteristics.
20. 5.29: Identifies story development, author's purpose, and point of view.

PLEASE GO ON TO THE NEXT PAGE.

In this passage the speaker describes what happens as day becomes night. To find out what happens when darkness falls, read the passage and answer the questions that follow.

Night Was Creeping
by James Stephens

The Night was creeping on the ground.
She crept and did not make a sound,

Until she reached the tree; and then
She covered it, and stole again

Along the grass beside the wall.
I heard the rustling of her shawl

As she threw blackness everywhere,
Along the sky, the ground, the air,

And in the room where I was hid.
But, no matter what she did

To everything that was without,
She could not put my candle out!

So I stared at the Night! And she
Stared <u>solemnly</u> back at me!

PLEASE GO ON TO THE NEXT PAGE. ⮑

21. How does the speaker feel about the Night?

    A. The speaker loves the Night.

    B. The speaker fears the Night.

    C. The speaker hopes the Night will never end.

    D. The speaker challenges the power of the Night.

    ⑥ **Tip:** Sometimes authors use descriptive words to show feelings. Skim back through the passage and look for clues to the author's feelings, such as the description of the Night's activities and the speaker's response.

22. What is the author's purpose in writing this passage?

    A. to persuade readers to stay indoors at night

    B. to warn readers about the dangers faced at night

    C. to describe nightfall using images

    D. to explain why it is important to have a candle at night

    ⑥ **Tip:** Authors express themselves in different ways for different purposes. Skim back through the passage. Notice the descriptive words and phrases. Decide whether the author wants to convince the reader of something, to inform the reader with factual information, or to entertain the reader with a creative way to think about night.

23. Which action is taken by both the Night and by the speaker in the poem?

    A. hiding

    B. staring

    C. creeping

    D. covering

    ⑥ **Tip:** Writers often make non-human things act like people in their stories or poems. The poet makes the Night into a human-like character. Look at all the actions the Night takes in the poem. Notice which action the Night and the speaker have in common.

24. Which word is an antonym of *solemnly*?

    A. seriously

    B. earnestly

    C. happily

    D. slyly

    ⑥ **Tip:** Antonyms are words that mean the opposite of one another. First consider what *solemnly* means. Then find the word that would be its opposite.

Georgia Reading Standards
21. **5.30:** Identifies characters' actions, motives, emotions, traits, and feelings.
22. **5.53:** Responds appropriately to questions about author's purpose, techniques, character development and plot structure.
23. **5.31:** Draws conclusions, makes predictions, compares/contrasts, and makes generalizations.
24. **5.37:** Uses knowledge of synonyms, antonyms, and homophones when reading.

Modeled Instruction
English/Language Arts

English/Language Arts has 31 questions and is divided into Section 1 and Section 2. For each question, choose the one best answer and circle the letter next to the answer.

1. What source would you use to find other words that mean the same thing as *curious*?

   A. a periodical

   B. an encyclopedia

   C. an atlas

   D. a thesaurus

   ⊙ **Tip:** Remember that a periodical is published at regular intervals. An encyclopedia has short, informative pieces. An atlas has maps. A thesaurus gives synonyms.

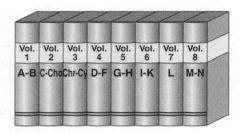

2. In what volume of an encyclopedia would you find information about China?

   A. Volume 1

   B. Volume 2

   C. Volume 3

   D. Volume 4

   ⊙ **Tip:** Alphabetical order can be more than using just the first letter of a word or name. Use the first, second, and third letters of the word *China* to find the correct answer.

figure¹ (fig'-yr) *n.* – **1.** a value or price

figure² (fig'-yr) *n.* – **1.** a shape, especially of a person **2.** a drawing that stands for a person, action, or object

figure³ (fig'-yr) *v.* – **1.** to calculate a solution to a math problem **2.** to decide

figure out (fig'-yr owt) *n.* – to find a solution to a problem

3. Based on the dictionary entry above, which meaning for *figure* fits the sentence in the box below?

   Erin could not buy the bicycle she wanted because the figure was too high.

   A. a value or price

   B. a drawing that stands for an object

   C. a shape, especially of a person

   D. a solution to a math problem

   ⊙ **Tip:** Many words have several meanings and may be different parts of speech. Notice that the word *figure* is used as a noun in the sentence. Think about which meaning is closest to the word as used in the sentence.

Georgia English/Language Arts Standards
1. **5.62:** Locates information using the appropriate reference sources.
2. **5.58:** Uses alphabetical order to locate information.
3. **5.60:** Uses dictionaries, thesauri, atlases, almanacs, periodicals, and encyclopedias to locate information.

PLEASE GO ON TO THE NEXT PAGE. ➲

Elena is gathering information about Georgia on the Internet. She wants to find information about the first colonists in Georgia.

4. Which key words should she type to get the most information?

    A. Georgia +history

    B. Georgia +geography

    C. Georgia +culture

    D Georgia +population

🌀 **Tip:** Using broad, general terms for Internet searches is the best way to find information. Think about what terms would be best applied to a search for the first colonists.

5. Which would you find in the index of a book?

    A. name of author and title of book

    B. chapter titles and their page numbers

    C. definitions of words in the book

    D. alphabetical list of different key terms and their page numbers

🌀 **Tip:** Most books have several specific parts. Review the divisions of a book. A title page lists the author and name of the book. A table of contents lists the chapter titles and page numbers. A glossary has definitions of words used in the book. An index lists key terms in alphabetical order and their page numbers. Decide which part would describe an index.

6. Which source should you use to find information about different breeds of dogs?

    A. a world atlas

    B. a dictionary

    C. an online reference

    D. an almanac

🌀 **Tip:** Different kinds of reference sources have particular information. A world atlas has a collection of different kinds of maps. A dictionary has information about words. An online reference would point to Web sites about particular information. An almanac gives information about individual states, such as population of cities and average rainfall. Think about which reference source would give the most information about dog breeds.

When the library opened, the students checked out _____ books.

7. What word correctly fills in the blank?

    A. they're

    B. there

    C. their

    D. thier

🌀 **Tip:** Some words sound alike, but are spelled differently and are used in different ways. Memorize the difference between a contraction (*they're*), an adverb (*there*), a possessive pronoun (*their*), and a word that is spelled incorrectly (*thier*).

Georgia English/Language Arts Standards
4. **5.64:** Uses research process by identifying key words.
5. **5.63:** Lists sources from which information is gathered, including author, title, publisher/producer, place of publication, and copyright date.
6. **5.59:** Uses the media center and available technology as sources of information and pleasure.
7. **5.78:** Spells frequently used words correctly and applies common spelling rules.

PLEASE GO ON TO THE NEXT PAGE. ➲

> We were late and <u>almost</u> missed the bus.

8. Which part of speech is the underlined word above?

   A. noun

   B. pronoun

   C. verb

   D. adverb

⑥ Tip: Parts of speech are the roles that words play in a sentence. A noun is the name of a person, place, or thing. A pronoun takes the place of a noun. A verb is an action word in the sentence. An adverb gives more information about the verb, an adjective, or another adverb. Reread the sentence and decide what role the underlined word plays in the sentence.

8. The guide words on a dictionary page are *groan* and *ground*. Which word would also be found on this page?

   A. grand

   B. gold

   C. gross

   D. gape

⑥ Tip: Dictionary guide words indicate what words may be found on a page. Since words in a dictionary are listed in alphabetical order, you must look at the first, second, and sometimes, third letter of words to figure out if they will appear on a page.

10. Which is a run-on sentence?

    A. Where are my shoes that I just bought yesterday?

    B. Alfred wants to go to his friend's house, but he has not finished his chores.

    C. Leslie went to school her dog got out of its pen and followed her.

    D. I went shopping today, but I did not buy anything.

⑥ Tip: Sentences have definite endings, such as question marks and periods. Sentences are run-on if they do not have a definite ending punctuation mark. Reread the sentences, and decide which one needs a definite ending.

11. Which sentence is punctuated correctly?

    A. Mike said I am going bird watching to find a "blue heron."

    B. I hope that "I make the team."

    C. Alicia said, "I saw a great movie this weekend."

    D. Dad said, "that he was cooking spaghetti tonight."

⑥ Tip: Sentences with quotations are punctuated according to rules. Remember that the introduction to the quote is followed by a comma. The quote is put inside quotation marks, and usually the sentence's end punctuation goes inside the quotation marks. Review the rules of punctuating quotations within sentences and decide which choice does follow the rules.

Georgia English/Language Arts Standards

8. **5.69:** Identifies at least five parts of speech, including nouns, verbs, pronouns, adjectives, and adverbs.
9. **5.61:** Uses guidewords to locate information.
10. **5.74:** Writes simple and compound sentences and avoids fragments and run-ons.
11. **5.77:** Applies standard rules of punctuation.

PLEASE GO ON TO THE NEXT PAGE. ➔

12. Which word in the sentence below needs to have a capital letter?

> Before Karen raced out the kitchen door, she told her mother that she was going to the park on State street.

   A. kitchen

   B. mother

   C. park

   D. street

Tip: Nouns may be common or proper. Proper nouns, such as the names of people and places, should always be capitalized. Review the sentence and decide what nouns are common and should not be capitalized. Then decide which noun is proper and should begin with a capital letter.

13. Which sentence below uses commas correctly?

   A. Latasha started, to feel tired but she did not want to go to bed.

   B. Latasha started to feel tired, but she did not want to go to bed.

   C. Latasha started to feel tired but she did not want, to go to bed.

   D. Latasha started to feel, tired but she did not want to go to bed

Tip: Commas may separate independent clauses if the independent clauses are joined by a word such as *and* or *but*. Reread the sentences and decide which sentence shows the correct use of a comma.

14. Which is a sentence fragment?

   A. Running around the block.

   B. Bill, pick up your room before company comes.

   C. Swimming on a swim team is fun in the summer.

   D. Although Spot heard Pat calling his name, he still looked for rabbits.

Tip: A complete sentence has a subject and a verb. A fragment usually looks like a sentence, but it doesn't have a verb to complete the thought. Reread the sentences and decide which one lacks a verb.

15. Which sentence correctly uses an adjective?

   A. Marie feels more better than she did yesterday.

   B. Sam was the most best runner in the fifth grade.

   C. Sarah has the best score in the class on the math test.

   D. James had the most better sandwich in his lunch box of anyone.

Tip: Remember that some adjectives have definite forms to show comparisons. For example, the comparative forms of the adjective *good* are *better* (for comparisons between two items) and *best* (for comparisons between more than two items). Read each sentence carefully and choose the correct form.

Georgia English/Language Arts Standards
12. **5.76:** Applies standard rules of capitalization.
13. **5.77:** Applies standard rules of punctuation.
14. **5.74:** Writes simple and compound sentences and avoids fragments and run-ons.
15. **5.75:** Applies standard conventions of American English in comparisons of adjectives and adverbs.

PLEASE GO ON TO THE NEXT PAGE. ➜

> Before Ella went to school, she braided her little sister's hair.

16. Which is a verb in the sentence above?

   A. Before

   B. school

   C. braided

   D. hair

🌀 **Tip:** Remember, a verb is an action word or a being word. It tells the action or the state of being for the subject of the sentence. A verb usually follows the subject of the sentence. Reread the sentence and decide which words are the subject and the verb of the main part of the sentence.

> When I arrived at the theater, my friends had already begun practicing their _____ for the play.

17. Which word correctly fills in the blank in the sentence above?

   A. roles

   B. role's

   C. roles'

   D. role'

🌀 **Tip:** To form the plural of nouns, add an –s or –es. The possessive form of a noun adds an 's for a singular noun. Reread the sentence and notice the difference between the plural form (more than one) of a noun and the possessive form (belonging to someone). Decide which form would best fill the blank.

18. Which sentence contains a FUTURE TENSE verb?

   A. I like to eat popcorn as a snack every time I watch a movie.

   B. Sandy used to like fish, but now he likes dogs as pets.

   C. Samantha says that she will like the color of her new room.

   D. I have liked to watch the Olympics every time I have seen them on television.

🌀 **Tip:** Future tense of a verb usually uses the helper words *shall* or *will* as part of the verb. Reread the sentences and decide which uses the helper words.

19. Which sentence is correctly capitalized?

   A. Soccer is my Favorite Game.

   B. The olympics are in athens, greece.

   C. The sign said "eat at joe's," so we ate there.

   D. Our class is singing "America" for our next assembly.

🌀 **Tip:** Remember that proper nouns are most often capitalized. Examples of proper nouns are the names of cities, states, and towns; names; and titles of songs. Read each sentence carefully and choose the correct one.

Georgia English/Language Arts Standards
16. **5.69:** Identifies at least five parts of speech, including nouns, verbs, pronouns, adjectives, and adverbs.
17. **5.71:** Forms singular, plural, and possessive nouns.
18. **5.72:** Identifies principal parts and tenses of regular and irregular verbs.
19. **5.63:** Applies standard rules of capitalization.

STOP!

Section 2

Modeled Instruction
English/Language Arts

Raquel and _____ went to see the play at school.

20. Which pronoun would BEST complete the sentence?

    A. me

    B. myself

    C. I

    D. us

🌀 **Tip:** A pronoun is a word that can take the place of a noun. The pronoun should match the noun in its use in the sentence. Reread the sentence and decide which pronoun matches the subject *Raquel*.

Ravi _____ across town to visit his grandparents yesterday.

21. Which verb correctly fills in the blank?

    A. went

    B. gone

    C. has gone

    D. will go

🌀 **Tip:** Verbs have several tenses that show when the action in a sentence takes place. Each tense is formed in a special way. For example, future tense uses the words *will* or *shall* to form its tense. Look for clues in the sentence that tell you when the action took place.

Sean <u>quickly</u> put away his favorite game when the school bell rang.

22. Which part of speech is the underlined word in the sentence above?

    A. noun

    B. adverb

    C. pronoun

    D. adjective

🌀 **Tip:** Parts of speech are the roles that words play in a sentence. An adverb gives more information about a verb, an adjective, or another adverb. A pronoun is a word that can replace a noun. A noun is the name of a person, place, or thing. An adjective describes a noun. Reread the sentence and think about how the word *quickly* is used in the sentence.

Each of Chuck's parents _____ to the meeting.

23. Which verb correctly fills the blank?

    A. is coming

    B. are coming

    C. were coming

    D. have been coming

🌀 **Tip:** Remember that subjects and verbs must agree in a sentence. The subject of this sentence is singular (*Each*). Choose the singular verb to agree with the subject.

Georgia English/Language Arts Standards

20. **5.73:** Identifies types of pronouns: subject, object, and possessive.
21. **5.72:** Identifies principal parts and tenses of regular and irregular verbs.
22. **5.69:** Identifies at least five parts of speech, including nouns, verbs, pronouns, adjectives, and adverbs.
23. **5.75:** Applies standard conventions of American English in subject-verb agreement.

PLEASE GO ON TO THE NEXT PAGE. ➡

Sharks are amazing fish that come in many different sizes and shapes. Sharks live all over the world. They can be found in every ocean and even in some rivers. My friend George saw a shark on his vacation. Unlike most other fish, sharks have to keep moving in order to stay afloat.

24. Which sentence is NOT related to the main idea of the paragraph?

    A. Sharks live all over the world.

    B. They can be found in every ocean and even in some rivers.

    C. My friend George saw a shark on his vacation.

    D. Unlike most other fish, sharks have to keep moving in order to stay afloat.

    ⓢ **Tip:** A paragraph usually has a topic sentence and supporting details. The details relate to the topic sentence directly to develop its information. Skim the paragraph and decide which sentence does not relate to the topic sentence.

25. Which is a complete sentence?

    A. The frightened horses ran outside.

    B. Sofia's red shoes with the buckles.

    C. Just before I returned home last night.

    D. Even though it all seemed like a dream.

    ⓢ **Tip:** A complete sentence has a subject and a predicate. A sentence fragment will only tell you who or what the sentence is about, or what happened, but not both.

The large, plump dodo bird had small wings and short legs that caused it to waddle.

26. Which of the underlined words is NOT as descriptive as the others?

    A. plump

    B. small

    C. short

    D. caused

    ⓢ **Tip:** Descriptive words may be adjectives that tell more about nouns. Reread the sentence and decide which of the underlined words is not an adjective.

27. Between which two guide words in an encyclopedia would information on the Egypt be found?

    A. *Earth* and *Ecuador*

    B. *Edward* and *Elizabeth*

    C. *East Pakistan* and *Egeria*

    D. *El Greco* and *Empire State*

    ⓢ **Tip:** Guide words can help you find information because they indicate an alphabetical order. Sometimes you have to look at the second or third letter in a word to find the correct guide words. Compare the spelling of *Egypt* to each set of guide words and choose the correct answer.

Georgia English/Language Arts Standards
24. **5.46:** Communicates by using the writing process: focuses on topic.
25. **5.74:** Writes simple and compound sentences and avoids fragments and run-on sentences.
26. **5.48:** Uses descriptive words and phrases.
27. **5.61:** Uses guide words to locate information.

PLEASE GO ON TO THE NEXT PAGE. ➔

22 ● Modeled Instruction

28. What type of sentence is the one below?

> If the mail is delivered early, I can check the mailbox for Aunt Laura's letter.

A. declarative

B. imperative

C. interrogative

D. exclamatory

🌀 **Tip:** Different kinds of sentences have different purposes. A declarative states information, an imperative gives commands, an interrogative asks questions, and an exclamatory sentence shows surprise. Think about what kind of information a sentence provides to decide what type it is.

29. Which word in the sentence below is a plural noun?

> Once on our vacation, about twenty sheep stopped our car on the highway.

A. vacation

B. sheep

C. car

D. highway

🌀 **Tip:** Some words, such as *deer* and *moose*, have plurals that are the same form as the singular. Reread the sentence and decide which word is the same in both its singular and plural forms.

> Unfortunately, Quinn _____ his bicycle pump and was unable to fix the tire.

30. Which verb correctly fills in the blank?

A. loses

B. lost

C. lose

D. losing

🌀 **Tip:** Verbs must match the tense of the sentence. Consider whether the action takes place in the past, present, or future. Then choose the correct verb.

> Tanisha wants to make breakfast for her family. _____, she needs to decide what to cook.

31. Which transition word would BEST complete the sentence?

A. First

B. Next

C. Then

D. Last

🌀 **Tip:** Steps in a sequence may have clue words, such as *first*, *next*, *then*, and *finally*. Decide which step would fit in the blank to show the process, and choose the word that matches.

Georgia English/Language Arts Standards

28. **5.68:** Identifies the types of sentences according to purpose: declarative, interrogative, imperative, and exclamatory.

29. **5.71:** Forms singular, plural, and possessive nouns.

30. **5.75:** Applies standard conventions of American English in: subject-verb agreement, cases of personal pronouns, principal parts of verbs, comparisons of adjectives and adverbs.

31. **5.46:** Communicates ideas by using the writing process: Improves sequence.

Now you are ready to take the Practice Test for the CRCT in Reading and English/Language Arts. Use what you learned in the first section of this book to help you succeed on this test.

Try using the following tips as you take the Practice Test:

- Read the directions carefully. Ask your teacher to explain anything that you do not understand.

- Read each passage carefully. Read each question and all the answer choices carefully. As you answer the question, you may look back at the reading selection as often as necessary.

- For the multiple-choice questions, fill in the circle next to the best answer choice on the answer sheet. Be sure to fill in the circle completely. If you want to change your answer, be sure to erase your first answer completely.

- If you are having trouble answering a question, skip it and go on to the next question. You may return to it later if you have time.

- If you don't know the answer right away, get rid of the answer choices you know are wrong. Take your best guess from the ones that remain.

- If you finish the section of the test that you are working on early, you may review your answers in that section only. You may not go on to the next section of the test.

Sometimes people worry when they take a test. Try to remember what you have learned about taking tests. Knowing what to expect should help you feel more confident and improve your score.

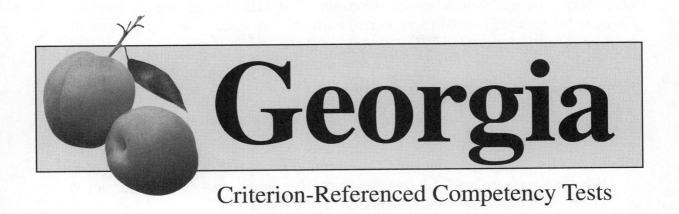

Criterion-Referenced Competency Tests

Reading and English/Language Arts Grade 5 Practice Test

READING

Directions: You will now be taking a Reading Test with multiple-choice questions. Go over the sample question so you will know how to mark your answers on the answer sheet. Read the following directions before beginning.

Keep these important points in mind:

1 Carefully read each passage. You may look back at the reading passage as needed.

2 Carefully read each question and then think about the answer. Choose the best answer, and fill in the circle for your answer on your answer sheet. Do not mark your answers in the book.

3 If you are having trouble with the answer to a question, skip it and go on to the next question. You may go back to it later if you have time.

4 Be sure to mark all of your answers on the answer sheet.

PLEASE GO ON TO THE NEXT PAGE. ➔

Sample Question

Below is a sample test question. This will show you what the questions in the test are like and how to mark your answer to each question. For each question in the test, choose the best answer and fill in the circle on your answer sheet for the answer you have chosen.

Flavor Favorites

Who doesn't like chocolate bars and vanilla ice cream? These flavors have been favorites for hundreds of years. Once only powerful and wealthy people enjoyed them. When Hernán Cortés visited the Aztecs in the early 1600s, they honored their guest by feeding him chocolate. The Aztecs believed that chocolate was a gift from a wise god.

Chocolate was the drink of Aztec kings and warriors. They drank it unsweetened, often mixing in chili peppers. When Cortés brought chocolate back to Europe, people added sugar to it. Then they couldn't get enough of it! He also brought back vanilla, which the Aztecs sometimes used to flavor their chocolate. Vanilla grew only in rain forests, so vanilla-craving Europeans had to pay a lot for it. Chocolate and vanilla were still treats for the wealthy.

Today, you can enjoy these flavors in many foods. And you don't even have to be king or a millionaire!

In this passage, the word <u>craving</u> means

A. afraid.

B. against.

C. desiring.

D. full.

PLEASE GO ON TO THE NEXT PAGE. ➡

READING

Section 1 of this test has twenty questions. After you read each passage, choose the best answer for each question. Fill in the circle for questions 1 through 20 on your answer sheet.

In this passage, a grandmother tells a fairy tale. To find out what makes this fairy tale unusual, read the passage and answer the questions that follow.

The Castle

"A long time ago in a land far away, there was a queen and a castle. The castle had all the things that make castles wonderful, like a drawbridge and a moat, but it was empty then. I don't remember who found the castle, but I'm sure that whoever it was ran right home to tell the others."

"Where did you find such a wonderful place?" Jenna asked.

"Oh, it wasn't wonderful at first," her grandmother answered. "But we moved in as soon as we discovered it, and in no time at all it had lace curtains, a velvet carpet, and a window to the sky."

"But where *was* the castle?" Ricky asked.

"In the forest, of course," his grandmother answered. "It got very dark there, and animals came around from time to time."

"Weren't you afraid?" Jenna asked.

"I had my knights in shining armor to protect me," her grandmother said. "Sometimes I protected them, too!" she added, laughing a bit. "We always took care of each other."

"What did the knights look like?" Ricky asked. Ricky imagined them just like the knights of King Arthur.

His grandmother got out some pictures. She flipped through them.

"Here are my knights," she said smiling, showing a picture to the children.

There were two boys in the photograph, dressed all in gray. They were tramping through the forest in big black boots. In the background stood the castle. The grandmother explained that they had to straighten the carpet each time one of them lifted up the boards they used for a drawbridge and climbed up the ladder they had placed on the large, thick trunk.

"Where is the queen?" Jenna asked, quite delighted with her grandmother's story. The old woman just smiled. The children knew that the queen was right in front of them, telling stories.

PLEASE GO ON TO THE NEXT PAGE. ➡

1. What did the author think you might have known before you read the passage?

   A. Where the grandmother lived

   B. Who King Arthur was

   C. Why the castle is in the forest

   D. What the grandmother did when she was young

2. Why did the grandmother decide to move into the "castle"?

   A. It had knights.

   B. It needed carpet.

   C. It looked dark.

   D. It was empty.

3. What is it that Ricky and Jenna's grandmother calls a castle?

   A. The house where she lived

   B. A building down the street

   C. A treehouse in the woods

   D. A palace she visited

4. Which of the following helps you understand that the castle was a real place?

   A. The castle was made of stone.

   B. The castle had boards for a drawbridge.

   C. The castle can be seen in a photograph.

   D. The castle was built a long time ago.

5. Grandmother's tone as she tells the story shows that she

   A. had a good imagination.

   B. was a lonely child.

   C. believed she was a queen.

   D. did not know what was real.

PLEASE GO ON TO THE NEXT PAGE. ➔

This passage presents information about an upcoming event. To find out how Town History Day will be celebrated, read the passage and answer the questions that follow.

North Central School's
Town History Day
October 14

About Town History Day

- North Central School's Town History Day is a fun way to learn about our town.

- Local historians will act out events from our town's past.

- Students will have a chance to win prizes by answering town history <u>trivia</u> questions. Start now to find out every small, insignificant detail about the early days of our town. Then watch the play for more information about the founding of our town.

How to Take Part

Any student in grades 5 through 8 can take part in Town History Day.

- Sign up on the list outside of Ms. Minh's classroom.

- Participating students will report to the gym to watch the play and take notes.

- Enter the trivia contest and win prizes by answering town history questions.

Prizes will be awarded based on the number of correct answers.

Number of Correct Answers	Prize
1–5	town map
6–10	town history book
11–15	town history encyclopedia
16 or more	town history book town history encyclopedia meeting with the mayor

Sign up today and learn about your hometown!

PLEASE GO ON TO THE NEXT PAGE.

6. What should you do first to take part in Town History Day?

   A. sign the list

   B. go to the gym

   C. watch the play

   D. answer questions

7. In this passage, the word *trivia* means

   A. useful.

   B. unimportant.

   C. humorous.

   D. serious.

8. What is the BEST reason for the school to support Town History Day?

   A. encourage historians to act

   B. teach students about their town

   C. host a trivia contest on October 14

   D. get students to visit Ms. Minh's classroom

9. A student who answers seven questions correctly will receive

   A. a town map.

   B. a town history book.

   C. a town history encyclopedia.

   D. a town history book and encyclopedia.

10. What was the author's purpose for creating this poster for Town History Day?

   A. to get historians involved

   B. to describe last year's event

   C. to persuade students to attend

   D. to share information about the event

PLEASE GO ON TO THE NEXT PAGE. ➡

The deep ocean is a dark, strange place. To find out about the amazing animals that live there, read the passage and answer the questions that follow.

Deep-Sea Monsters

Maybe you've watched an old black-and-white film, with its slimy swamp monster. Or you might have seen the latest sci-fi flick, starring aliens with pale, bulging eyes in sets of four. But you haven't seen the strangest creatures until you look deep into Earth's oceans, where odd life forms abound.

That creatures live in the deepest ocean is odd in itself. No diver has ever been down so far, but special submarines that have explored the ocean thousands of feet down have sent back pictures of a <u>harsh</u> environment. Almost no sunlight filters down to these black waters, and temperatures are <u>frigid</u>, except where volcanic vents spew hot gas and water from beneath the ocean floor. Scientists are amazed by how many life forms have adapted to these icy waters.

To live, fish need to hunt and eat. Hunters use their eyes to find food. The lack of light at these depths has caused fish to develop huge eyes to catch the few rays that do reach them. Fish are also looking for a different sort of light—a light produced by other fish. The dragonfish, for example, has light-producing organs in rows on its sides and glowing fins that attract fish that the dragonfish eats. Viper fish, whose long, sharp, pale teeth look quite vicious, have lights inside their mouths to lure fish in. Chemically lit fish attract both hunters and prey in this dark world.

Big eyes and big teeth are a great help, but a big mouth and a big stomach are good, too. In this ocean underworld, dinner doesn't swim by every day. Some fish have learned to eat few but big meals. Small fish whose jaws open wide can swallow prey twice their size. One such fish, the gulper eel, looks like something out of a particularly horrible sci-fi movie. A skinny fish with a little red light on its tail, the gulper eel can gulp down fish three times its size. Its flexible skeleton handles the pressure of deep water. When the gulper eel catches prey, dozens of sharp teeth drag the fish into its stomach, which can double in size. This way, the eel can live for quite some time before it must eat again.

Scientists once thought that nothing could survive on the floor of the abyss, more than two miles under the ocean's surface. But strange creatures live here, too. Many live on bits of dead fish that float down from above. Tripod fish stand on three long fins, waiting to catch deep-sea shrimp. But oddest of all are the tubeworms, some as tall as an adult human, that crowd around the volcanic vents. The vents churn out steaming black water filled with a gas that smells like rotten eggs. Bacteria that thrive on the gas live in the tubeworms' bodies, where the tubeworms eat them.

Does all this sound like science fiction? If so, brace yourself: Scientists say that we have not yet met many of the ocean's strange citizens.

PLEASE GO ON TO THE NEXT PAGE. ➲

11. What does the gulper eel use its sharp teeth for?

    A.   to attract prey

    B.   to collect bacteria

    C.   to pull food into its stomach

    D.   to handle the pressure of deep water

12. Which sentence expresses a conclusion based on the passage?

    A.   Deep ocean creatures all glow in the dark.

    B.   Scientists send divers down to study the bacteria.

    C.   Studying the deep ocean yields many surprises.

    D.   Volcanic vents warm the deep ocean waters.

13. In this passage, the word *frigid* means

    A.   very dark.

    B.   extremely cold.

    C.   comfortably warm.

    D.   quick to change.

14. Which word is an antonym of *harsh*?

    A.   familiar

    B.   bright

    C.   pleasant

    D.   dark

PLEASE GO ON TO THE NEXT PAGE. ➜

> *This story is about students who want to start a school paper. To find out how they plan to begin the task, read the passage and answer the questions that follow.*

Start the Presses!

One afternoon Rafael ran into Miki, who was reading the notices on a bulletin board. "You know, this drives me nuts!" Miki said, before she even said hello. "I can't remember all the information on these notices. How am I supposed to know what's going on in this school?"

"We need a school paper." Rafael said. "Then we'd know what was going on."

"That's a great idea," Miki grinned. "Our school has never had a newspaper, but we could put one together. But what should we write? And how will we get it printed?"

After school, Miki and Rafael sat outside, waiting for the bus and brainstorming about their new project. "I was thinking we could write about things happening around school," Miki suggested early on. "Maybe we could even have stories about great teachers or really good students."

"That and sports," Rafael said. "But I've been thinking that researching, interviewing, and writing all these stories is going to be a lot of work!"

"Well, maybe we'll have to start smaller, with a newsletter." Miki was still excited about the idea, but the more she and Rafael talked, the more worried she was that there were too many tasks. She was beginning to think that the whole thing seemed too big to distribute between just the two of them.

"Hey." Ren was standing by them. "I heard you talking about a newspaper. The school I came from had one, and I wrote for it. I'd like to help on this one, too."

"Great!" said Rafael, with relief. "Where do we start?"

"The best thing to do is pick a subject and get busy. Tell you what—you know the new social studies teacher, Ms. Owens?" Rafael and Miki nodded. "She just spent a year living and teaching in Japan. That's a good story."

"Good idea, Ren. I'll start a story about the fundraiser for the library. Rafael—sports?" Miki asked.

Over the next few days, the writers went to work. Miki talked to the librarian and a parent who was in charge of the library fundraiser. She found out the date, time, place, and other details. Miki promised that the newsletter would come out in time for the fundraiser. She and the librarian wanted as many students to participate as possible and for the fundraiser to be a success.

Rafael looked in the gym after school. There he spotted Coach Russell in his office.

"Coach Russell?" Rafael asked as he knocked politely on the door. "Would you be interested in putting some information about the school's sports teams in a newspaper we're trying to start?"

Coach Russell smiled. "Of course, Rafael," he said. "What a great idea for us to remind students of all the upcoming events they could participate in or all the after-school clubs that they could join. I'd be happy to."

Ren interviewed Ms. Owens. He wanted to talk to her to find out more information about her stay in Japan. When Ren and Ms. Owens talked, Ren learned that Ms. Owens had

PLEASE GO ON TO THE NEXT PAGE.

always wanted to travel in the Far East. When she graduated from college she applied for a job teaching overseas. She was able to teach at a special school in Tokyo. There she studied the Japanese culture and made a special study of Japan's arts and crafts. Ms. Owens showed Ren some of her photographs. Together they thought about how the photographs might also appear in the newspaper.

"Thanks for telling my story, Ren," Ms. Owens said as Ren shut his notebook. "I like the idea of a school paper. But your paper needs a faculty sponsor to help you get it printed and handed out. I'd be glad to do that."

When Ren told Rafael and Miki about Ms. Owens's offer to help, Miki smiled. "She's right—we will need help sometimes. It's always good to look for others who want to get involved. Like you and Rafael, and now Ms. Owens."

15. Why do Miki and Rafael decide to start a school newspaper?

A. Rafael wants to write about sports.

B. Their school has never had a newspaper.

C. They want to know what is going on at their school.

D. Ms. Owens suggests that the students start a newspaper.

16. Which of these words from the passage is a compound word?

A. library

B. between

C. fundraiser

D. interviewing

17. This passage is an example of

    A. a class report.

    B. a diary entry.

    C. a fictional story.

    D. a news story.

18. Which word means the same thing as *distribute*?

    A. create

    B. divide

    C. show

    D. write

19. Which sentence states the main idea of the story?

    A. School newspapers need interesting stories.

    B. Every school newspaper needs a faculty sponsor.

    C. It is always a good idea to work with others.

    D. Big jobs sometimes require help to do them.

20. How did Miki feel at the end of the passage?

    A. worried

    B. serious

    C. encouraged

    D. nervous

PLEASE STOP! DO NOT GO ON TO THE NEXT PAGE. STOP!

READING

Section 2 of this test has twenty questions. Read each passage and choose the best answer for each question. Fill in the circle for questions 21 through 40 on your answer sheet.

The following passage describes the speaker's first bicycle. To find out what the bicycle meant to the speaker, read the passage and answer the questions that follow.

The Blue Bicycle

I was ten when I saw it,
the blue bicycle gleaming on the sidewalk,
sleek and trim,
ready for riding!

I was ten when I felt it,
the snug fit of the white helmet,
reflectors announcing me
to the open road!

Thousands of pennies not spent on candy,
pounds of dimes earned raking leaves,
pile after pile of quarters,
one blue bicycle!

How I remember that day,
when joy tugged me up,
and I first glimpsed the trail
of journeys never made before!

21. What did the speaker do first in the passage?

   A. buy the bicycle

   B. see the bicycle

   C. save money for the bicycle

   D. ride the bicycle

22. Which word is a synonym for *glimpsed*?

   A. traveled

   B. dreamed

   C. saw

   D. rode

23. The author's purpose in writing this passage is to

   A. convince readers to save money

   B. describe for readers a joyful event

   C. explain to readers about bike safety

   D. persuade readers to buy bicycles

24. This passage is an example of

   A. a drama

   B. a report

   C. a story

   D. a poem

PLEASE GO ON TO THE NEXT PAGE. ➲

This is the story of man who became an important leader. To find out who this man was and what he did, read the passage and answer the questions that follow.

A Man of Peace

In 1929 a man of peace was born in Atlanta, Georgia. The son and grandson of Baptist preachers, he was expected to follow in their footsteps. Beginning the first grade when he was only five years old, this young man did very well throughout his school days. He skipped the ninth and twelfth grades, and entered college when he was only 15.

He graduated in 1948 from Morehouse College and enrolled in the seminary to become a minister. Elected president of his senior class, he won the first of many awards, this one for being the most outstanding student. Still hungry for knowledge, he attended Boston University and Harvard, earning his Ph.D. in 1955.

His ministry began at a church in Montgomery, Alabama. Then in 1960, he moved back home to Atlanta to become head of the Southern Christian Leadership Conference.

During the 1950s and 1960s, African Americans wanted equal treatment under the law. He would guide them in their struggle. But rather than using force, the minister tried to help them reach their goals through peaceful means. He and his followers would peacefully argue against unfair laws. At times, he and his followers were met by angry crowds, but they were determined to remain peaceful.

Using his ideas, African Americans brought attention to their fight for equality. Their efforts ended segregation on buses in Montgomery, Alabama. It also encouraged many people around the country to support the African American cause. In 1963 he led a march on Washington, D.C. Over 200,000 people marched to show that African Americans deserve to be treated as equals.

He was always a dynamic speaker. One of his famous speeches is "I Have a Dream," which he delivered on the steps of the Lincoln Memorial. In the speech, he inspires his listeners to dream of a day when all people will be judged "not by the color of their skin, but by the content of their character."

This man of peace was awarded the Nobel Peace Prize in 1964. Today, Americans celebrate his birthday on the third Monday of every January. As you may have already guessed, this man of peace is Dr. Martin Luther King, Jr.

PLEASE GO ON TO THE NEXT PAGE. ⮕

25. Which of the following is an opinion?

A. He would guide them in their struggle.

B. He was always a dynamic speaker.

C. In 1963 he led a march on Washington, D.C.

D. This man of peace was awarded the Nobel Peace Prize in 1964.

26. According to the passage, which of the following BEST describes Dr. King?

A. an honest minister

B. an angry man

C. a peaceful leader

D. a loving son

27. This passage was written to provide the reader with information about

A. a cultural hero

B. the Nobel Peace Prize

C. our sixteenth president

D. the history of Civil Rights

28. The author's purpose in writing this passage is to

A. to describe Dr. King's appearance.

B. to give important details about Dr. King's life.

C. to persuade readers to admire Dr. King.

D. to entertain readers with stories about Dr. King.

29. Which sentence tells what happened first in the passage?

A. Martin Luther King became a minister.

B. Martin Luther King fought for African American equality.

C. Martin Luther King was an excellent student.

D. Martin Luther King won a Nobel Prize.

30. Which word is a synonym for *fight*?

A. segregation

B. treatment

C. struggle

D. means

PLEASE GO ON TO THE NEXT PAGE. ➡

This passage describes the Appalachian Trail. To learn why people are attracted to this challenging hiking route, read the passage and answer the questions that follow.

The Appalachian Trail

Did you know that a hiking trail over 2,000 miles long runs into Georgia? The trail is the Appalachian Trail. It stretches as far north as Mount Katahdin, Maine. From Maine, the trail heads south along the Appalachian Mountains. It reaches as far south as Springer Mountain, Georgia. In all, the Appalachian Trail passes through 14 states.

Benton MacKaye, a forester from Massachusetts, first proposed the Appalachian Trail. Volunteers helped to get it ready to open in 1837. Today more than 4,000 volunteers take care of the trail. Almost 100% of the land itself is owned and protected by the state or federal governments.

So how long does it take to hike the Appalachian Trail? If you hiked 15 miles a day, it would take about 137 days. That's about 4.5 months! No wonder so many people only hike only part of the trail. People hiking the entire trail must carry equipment with them. They need food, water, clothes, a tent, and a sleeping bag. Hikers can pick up some of this equipment in towns along the trail. Even so, they must plan ahead or their hike can be very difficult.

If it is so difficult, why do people hike the Appalachian Trail? The trail offers people a chance to spend time in nature. It passes through eight national forests and two national parks. Hikers on the trail can look out from the tops of mountains. They can follow the rivers that shaped the land. They can see all sorts of plants and wildlife that they've never seen before. Most of all, when the hike is finished, hikers feel a sense of pride at having <u>conquered</u> such a long trail.

PLEASE GO ON TO THE NEXT PAGE. ➔

31. In this passage, the word *conquered* means

    A.   approached.

    B.   completed.

    C.   defeated.

    D.   viewed.

32. Which of these words found in the passage is a compound word?

    A.   equipment

    B.   wildlife

    C.   national

    D.   difficult

33. Which would be another title for the passage?

    A.   *Georgia Attractions*

    B.   *A Trip Across the United States*

    C.   *The Hike of a Lifetime*

    D.   *The Appalachian Mountains*

34. This passage does NOT tell us that people hike the Appalachian Trail to

    A.   see many states in the trip.

    B.   complete a difficult task.

    C.   get from town to town.

    D.   spend 137 days walking.

35. Why do many people hike only part of the Appalachian Trail?

    A.   The whole trail takes more than four months to hike.

    B.   People have to carry all the food they will need.

    C.   The trail goes across fourteen states.

    D.   The trail is difficult.

PLEASE GO ON TO THE NEXT PAGE. ➔

The Dead Sea and the Great Salt Lake are two famous bodies of water. To find out what makes them so unusual, read the passage and answer the questions that follow.

Salty Waters

Many people think that inland lakes contain fresh water and oceans contain salt water. While that's mostly true, there are two famous inland lakes that are saltier than the oceans — so salty that almost nothing can survive in them. One of these lakes is in our nation: the Great Salt Lake of Utah. The other is halfway around the world: the Dead Sea, bordered by Jordan and Israel. The Dead Sea is the lowest body of water on Earth, over thirteen hundred feet below sea level.

Why are these inland bodies of water not fresh? Most lakes are fed by rivers and streams that flow into them, bringing not only water but also various minerals, such as salt. Most lakes empty into rivers and streams which finally find their way to the ocean, carrying minerals back out with them. The Great Salt Lake is fed by three rivers. The Dead Sea gets water mainly from the Jordan River. However, neither lake has an outlet—the water that flows in is trapped. It can leave the lakes in only one way, through evaporation. The water may evaporate, but it leaves its minerals behind. So the Great Salt Lake and the Dead Sea have become saltier and saltier over many centuries.

Many creatures live in the salty waters of Earth's oceans. But almost nothing can survive in the Dead Sea or the Great Salt Lake. Fish that swim into the Dead Sea from the Jordan River die right away. Only some salt-loving bacteria live in these lakes. The Dead Sea is in a desert; very little plant life lives near it. The Great Salt Lake's borders, on the other hand, are marshes and mudflats that provide homes for many types of birds.

Though both lakes sound like places unfriendly to humans, they are actually useful. Tourists go to the Dead Sea to indulge in salt treatments that soften the skin. They enjoy the odd experience of being able to lie down in the thick water and have it support them. People travel to the Great Salt Lake for the wildlife preserves around it, and to enjoy its white beaches and cool waters. Both lakes provide salt and many other minerals to industry. Both are strangely beautiful bodies of water that people can admire and study.

PLEASE GO ON TO THE NEXT PAGE. ➲

36. Which of these words from the passage is a contraction?

    A. tourists

    B. Lake's

    C. that's

    D. its

37. What is the main purpose of this passage?

    A. to tell readers a fiction story about salty water

    B. to convince readers to give up salt

    C. to inform readers about two salty bodies of water

    D. to describe for readers a swim in the Great Salt Lake

38. Which of the following is true of the Dead Sea?

    A. Its water flows into the ocean.

    B. It offers no practical uses for humans.

    C. It is located in the United States.

    D. It is located below sea level.

39. Why is the Dead Sea so salty?

    A. Evaporating water leaves behind minerals and salt.

    B. Industries dump salt into the water.

    C. More water flows out than flows in.

    D. It is not fed by any rivers.

40. How is the Dead Sea different from the Great Salt Lake?

    A. The Dead Sea is in a desert.

    B. Its waters are saltier than the Great Salt Lake.

    C. Bacteria can live in the Great Salt Lake but not the Dead Sea.

    D. The Dead Sea is home to many different birds and animals.

PLEASE STOP! DO NOT GO ON TO THE NEXT PAGE. STOP!

NO TEST MATERIAL
ON THIS PAGE

English/Language Arts
Grade 5
Practice Test

ENGLISH/LANGUAGE ARTS

Directions: You will now be taking an English/Language Arts test with multiple-choice questions. Go over the sample question so you will know how to mark your answers on the answer sheet.

Keep these important points in mind:

1 Carefully read each question and then think about the answer. Choose the best answer, and fill in the circle for your answer on your answer sheet. Do not mark your answers in the book.

2 If you are having trouble with the answer to a question, skip it and go on to the next question. You may go back to it later if you have time.

3 Be sure to mark all of your answers on the answer sheet.

PLEASE GO ON TO THE NEXT PAGE. ➡

Sample Question

Below is a sample test question. This will show you what the questions in the test are like and how to mark your answer to each question. For each question in the test, choose the best answer and fill in the circle on your answer sheet for the answer you have chosen.

Which word below is an example of a compound word?

A. also

B. carriage

C. sometime

D. distrust

ENGLISH/LANGUAGE ARTS

Section 1

Section 1 of this test has twenty-five questions. Choose the best answer for each question. Fill in the circle for questions 1 through 25 on your answer sheet.

In his paintings, Joan Miró used bright colors to pick out each object. He would focus on the curves that made up his subjects. In some of his art, background objects got most of the attention.

---

1. Which would make the best opening sentence for the paragraph?

   A. Joan Miró paid attention to background objects.

   B. Joan Miró began studying to be a painter in 1912.

   C. Joan Miró created a special style for his art.

   D. Joan Miró was interested in using bright, strong colors.

2. What type of sentence is the one below?

We must finish right away.

   A. declarative

   B. interrogative

   C. imperative

   D. exclamatory

Georgia is home to many different forms of art. Atlanta, Georgia, has museums and a school for the arts. Atlanta is the capital city. A skilled theater company calls Georgia home. In addition, different styles of music are popular across the state.

---

3. Which sentence does not belong in the paragraph?

   A. Georgia is home to many different forms of art.

   B. Atlanta is the capital city.

   C. A skilled theater company calls Georgia home.

   D. In addition, different styles of music are popular across the state.

The *artist* made many colorful paintings of the ocean.

---

4. Which of the underlined words is a modifier?

   A. artist

   B. colorful

   C. paintings

   D. ocean

PLEASE GO ON TO THE NEXT PAGE. ➡

5. Which of the following is a complete sentence?

   A. Tran wanted to go home.

   B. Until we got home.

   C. Something to think about.

   D. Sometimes when I study.

6. The guide words on a dictionary page are *hunger* and *hut*. Which word would be found on this page?

   A. humid

   B. humor

   C. hunch

   D. hush

7. What type of sentence is the one below?

   | Where are we going on our field trip? |

   A. declarative

   B. interrogative

   C. imperative

   D. exclamatory

8. In which part of a book would you find the meaning of a word?

   A. index

   B. title page

   C. table of contents

   D. glossary

9. The guide words on an encyclopedia page are *softball* and *Solomon Islands*. Which subject would be found on this page?

   A. snow leopard

   B. solar system

   C. sound

   D. soybean

PLEASE GO ON TO THE NEXT PAGE. ⮕

> You should oil the chain of a bicycle on a regular basis.

10. Which is a verb in the sentence above?

    A. You

    B. oil

    C. regular

    D. basis

> I didn't want to leave any of the cute little _____ alone.

11. What word BEST fills in the blank in the sentence above?

    A. puppys

    B. puppy's

    C. puppies

    D. puppies'

12. Which source would you use to find information about a camping area that is near your home?

    A. an outdoor adventure magazine

    B. a Web site of state campgrounds

    C. a book about camping in Europe

    D. a card catalog

> Jenna walked slowly toward the entrance.

13. Which part of speech is the underlined word in the sentence above?

    A. verb

    B. adjective

    C. pronoun

    D. adverb

14. Which sentence contains a FUTURE TENSE verb?

    A. I will go to the dentist on Monday.

    B. She went to school in spite of her headache.

    C. Frank goes hiking with his mom.

    D. My cousin has gone to the park.

PLEASE GO ON TO THE NEXT PAGE. ➡

When I stay at my grandmother's house, she lets me make dinner. I always make rice and beans. First, I put the rice and water in a pot on the stove. Then, I open a can of beans. I heat the beans slowly in a pan. Finally, when the rice and beans are ready, I serve them with some cheese. It is a quick and easy meal. Black beans are my favorite.

15. Which sentence does not belong in the paragraph?

    A. First, I put the rice and some water on the stove.

    B. I heat the beans slowly in a pan.

    C. Black beans are my favorite.

    D. It is a quick and easy meal.

16. What type of sentence is the one below?

Elena touched the hot stove and her hand is burned!

    A. declarative

    B. interrogative

    C. exclamatory

    D. imperative

17. Where should you look to find directions on making a birdhouse?

    A. an encyclopedia

    B. a book on crafts

    C. a thesaurus

    D. an almanac

PLEASE GO ON TO THE NEXT PAGE. ➡

18. Which encyclopedia volume above would you use to find the most information about Yellowstone National Park?

   A.   Volume 7

   B.   Volume 8

   C.   Volume 9

   D.   Volume 10

19. Which sentence is punctuated correctly?

   A.   "What time is it," asked Ahmed.

   B.   "What time is it" asked Ahmed?

   C.   "What time is it?" asked Ahmed.

   D.   "What time is it." asked Ahmed.

> **bean sprouts** *n.* – the sprouts of bean seeds
>
> **bear**[1] (ber) *n.* – **1.** a four-legged animal with shaggy fur and a small tail **2.** a person who is rude or has poor manners
>
> **bear**[2] (ber) *v.* – **1.** to carry or support **2.** to suffer or live with **3.** to have as a part
>
> **bearable** (ber´ə•bl) *adj.* – describes something that one is able to bear
>
> **beard** (bird) *n.* – hair that grows on the face of a male not including the mustache

> Sheila can be a bear when she is tired.

20. Based on the dictionary entry above, which definition is correct for the word *bear*?

   A.   a four-legged animal with shaggy fur

   B.   a person who has poor manners

   C.   to suffer or live with

   D.   to have as a part

21. Based on the dictionary entry above, which piece of information is found after the word *bearable*?

   A.   the definition

   B.   the pronunciation

   C.   the part of speech

   D.   the antonym for the word

PLEASE GO ON TO THE NEXT PAGE. ➜

> The green turtle is a type of sea turtle. The leatherback turtle is a type of sea turtle.

22. Which correctly combines the above sentences into one meaningful sentence?

    A. There are sea turtles called green turtles and turtles called leatherback turtles.

    B. The green turtle is a type of sea turtle, the leatherback turtle is a type of sea turtle.

    C. The green turtle is a type of sea turtle so is the leatherback turtle.

    D. The green turtle and the leatherback turtle are types of sea turtles.

23. Which word in the sentence below needs to have a capital letter?

    > "Where should I put the groceries, mom?" she called out to her mother from the next room.

    A. groceries

    B. mom

    C. she

    D. room

> Mrs. Lowe worked <u>hard</u> to create her wonderful garden.

24. Which part of speech is the underlined word above?

    A. verb

    B. adverb

    C. noun

    D. pronoun

> Loretta and _____ went to our friend's softball game.

25. Which word belongs in the sentence?

    A. I

    B. us

    C. me

    D. ours

PLEASE STOP! DO NOT GO ON TO THE NEXT PAGE. STOP!

Section 2

Section 2 of this test has twenty-five questions. Choose the best answer for each question. Fill in the circle in the spaces provided for questions 26 through 50 on your answer sheet.

My best friend and I are playing soccer after school. _____, we need to get our soccer gear together.

26. Which transition word BEST completes the sentence above?

    A. Last

    B. First

    C. Next

    D. Third

I wanted to see the Grand canyon, but then my brother told me that it was several states away.

27. Which word in the sentence above needs a capital letter?

    A. canyon

    B. my

    C. brother

    D. states

Amy decided to write a report about the famous musician Dizzy Gillespie. She read books and took plenty of notes.

28. What should Amy do next?

    A. write a first draft from her notes

    B. create an outline from her notes

    C. find more books on her topic

    D. ask questions about her topic

29. Which sentence below has a possessive pronoun?

    A. Whom should we invite to the party?

    B. Tammy will give the book to you.

    C. Milo left it on the bus.

    D. That pencil is mine.

30. Which source would you use to find synonyms?

    A. a thesaurus

    B. an atlas

    C. a dictionary

    D. an encyclopedia

PLEASE GO ON TO THE NEXT PAGE. ➜

All of the cereal _____ gone by the time I woke up.

31. Which verb BEST completes the sentence above?

   A. was

   B. is

   C. were

   D. will be

The guitar the violin and the bass are all string instruments.

32. Which is the correct punctuation for the sentence above?

   A. guitar and the violin and the bass

   B. guitar, the violin, the bass

   C. the guitar, the violin, and the bass

   D. the guitar the violin, and the bass

I want to read the latest book by my favorite author. _____, I will see if the library has a copy. If not, then I will borrow my friend's copy.

33. Which transition word BEST completes the sentence above?

   A. First

   B. Next

   C. After

   D. Last

34. Which sentence correctly uses capital letters?

   A. My favorite book is *Holes* by Louis Sachar.

   B. The Baseball Team won the last three games.

   C. sarah and luther went to see a movie.

   D. I used to live on Pine street but now I live on Main.

PLEASE GO ON TO THE NEXT PAGE. ➔

> Tryouts began this week for the school's basketball team. The coaches had us run the track and do exercises. We practiced after school for about an hour.

35. Which could be a sentence with supporting details for this paragraph?

    A. Coaches coach just one sport.

    B. We shot baskets and ran a scrimmage.

    C. Our school won first place in 2004.

    D. The principal comes to all the games.

36. David is interested in doing a report on fish. Which is a relevant subject that would help him narrow his topic?

    A. animals

    B. whales

    C. tropical fish

    D. ocean creatures

37. The four sentences below express the same idea. Which sentence BEST expresses this idea?

    A. In the classroom the visitor arrived before the final bell rang.

    B. Before the final bell rang, arrived in the classroom the visitor.

    C. The visitor arrived in the classroom before the final bell rang.

    D. The visitor before the final bell rang arrived in the classroom.

38. What type of sentence is the one below?

    > Have you ever been to Americus, Georgia?

    A. imperative

    B. interrogative

    C. exclamatory

    D. declarative

39. Which word in the sentence below is a plural noun?

    > Outside Ryan's window, a small herd of deer feed on the lawn.

    A. Ryan's

    B. window

    C. deer

    D. feed

40. Which sentence correctly uses an apostrophe?

    A. I haven't turned in my library book yet.

    B. We'rent you going to the beach today?

    C. Can you see the Adams'es house from the corner?

    D. Paul has'nt found his missing pet lizard.

PLEASE GO ON TO THE NEXT PAGE. ➡

Table of Contents

41. Which part of the Table of Contents above would be the best source for a recipe for an entire healthy dinner?

    A. Introduction

    B. Chapter 1 *Starting Out* section

    C. Chapter 2 *A Balance of Foods* section

    D. Chapter 3 *Meals* section

42. In the sentence below, which of the underlined words is a noun?

    > James and his family <u>wanted</u> to have a picnic <u>in</u> the <u>park</u>, but it started to rain when they <u>arrived</u>.

    A. wanted

    B. in

    C. park

    D. arrived

43. Using the index below, on which pages would information about tomatoes be found?

    > Nutrition
    >   fat content, 27–28
    >   food pyramid, 29–30
    >   fruits, 31–35
    >   tomatoes, *see* fruits,
    >   vegetables, 36–37

    A. pages 27–28

    B. pages 29–30

    C. pages 31–35

    D. pages 36–37

> There are not too many vegetables I like, but I know I _____ that one.

44. Which verb would BEST complete this sentence above?

    A. did liking

    B. liked

    C. like

    D. am liking

PLEASE GO ON TO THE NEXT PAGE. ➡

45. In the sentence below, which of the underlined words is used as a verb?

> I hoped that my older brother would help me work on my pitching.

   A. hoped

   B. older

   C. me

   D. pitching

46. Using the listings for the library sections below, which library section would you choose to find a book about Georgia in the 1700s?

300	Social Sciences
400	Language
500	Science
600	Technology
700	Arts
800	Literature
900	History, Geography

   A. 300

   B. 400

   C. 700

   D. 900

47. Which would be the best source for gathering information about the history of the Cherokee people?

   A. a dictionary

   B. a thesaurus

   C. an encyclopedia

   D. a magazine

PLEASE GO ON TO THE NEXT PAGE. ➲

Mr. Harmon worried that the two _____ project might be too difficult.

48. Which word should fill in the blank in the sentence above?

A. student's

B. students

C. studentes

D. students'

Holly began her trip to <u>Atlanta Georgia on July 23 2004</u>.

49. Which sentence below uses commas correctly?

A. Holly began her trip to Atlanta Georgia, on July 23 2004.

B. Holly began her trip to Atlanta, Georgia on July, 23 2004.

C. Holly began her trip to Atlanta, Georgia, on July 23, 2004.

D. Holly began her trip to Atlanta Georgia on July 23, 2004.

The tallest boy on the basketball team made all the baskets.

50. In the sentence above, what is the verb?

A. tallest

B. team

C. made

D. baskets

PLEASE STOP! DO NOT GO ON TO THE NEXT PAGE. STOP!

READING TEST ANSWER SHEET

Name _____

Directions: Use this answer sheet for the multiple-choice questions. Fill in the circle for each correct answer.

Reading, Section 1

Sample (A) (B) (C) (D)

1. (A) (B) (C) (D)
2. (A) (B) (C) (D)
3. (A) (B) (C) (D)
4. (A) (B) (C) (D)
5. (A) (B) (C) (D)
6. (A) (B) (C) (D)
7. (A) (B) (C) (D)
8. (A) (B) (C) (D)
9. (A) (B) (C) (D)
10. (A) (B) (C) (D)
11. (A) (B) (C) (D)
12. (A) (B) (C) (D)
13. (A) (B) (C) (D)
14. (A) (B) (C) (D)
15. (A) (B) (C) (D)
16. (A) (B) (C) (D)
17. (A) (B) (C) (D)
18. (A) (B) (C) (D)
19. (A) (B) (C) (D)
20. (A) (B) (C) (D)

Reading, Section 2

21. (A) (B) (C) (D)
22. (A) (B) (C) (D)
23. (A) (B) (C) (D)
24. (A) (B) (C) (D)
25. (A) (B) (C) (D)
26. (A) (B) (C) (D)
27. (A) (B) (C) (D)
28. (A) (B) (C) (D)
29. (A) (B) (C) (D)
30. (A) (B) (C) (D)
31. (A) (B) (C) (D)
32. (A) (B) (C) (D)
33. (A) (B) (C) (D)
34. (A) (B) (C) (D)
35. (A) (B) (C) (D)
36. (A) (B) (C) (D)
37. (A) (B) (C) (D)
38. (A) (B) (C) (D)
39. (A) (B) (C) (D)
40. (A) (B) (C) (D)

ENGLISH/LANGUAGE ARTS TEST ANSWER SHEET

Name _____

Directions: Use this answer sheet for the multiple-choice questions. Fill in the circle for each correct answer.

English/Language Arts, Section 1

Sample Ⓐ Ⓑ Ⓒ Ⓓ

1. Ⓐ Ⓑ Ⓒ Ⓓ
2. Ⓐ Ⓑ Ⓒ Ⓓ
3. Ⓐ Ⓑ Ⓒ Ⓓ
4. Ⓐ Ⓑ Ⓒ Ⓓ
5. Ⓐ Ⓑ Ⓒ Ⓓ
6. Ⓐ Ⓑ Ⓒ Ⓓ
7. Ⓐ Ⓑ Ⓒ Ⓓ
8. Ⓐ Ⓑ Ⓒ Ⓓ
9. Ⓐ Ⓑ Ⓒ Ⓓ
10. Ⓐ Ⓑ Ⓒ Ⓓ
11. Ⓐ Ⓑ Ⓒ Ⓓ
12. Ⓐ Ⓑ Ⓒ Ⓓ
13. Ⓐ Ⓑ Ⓒ Ⓓ
14. Ⓐ Ⓑ Ⓒ Ⓓ
15. Ⓐ Ⓑ Ⓒ Ⓓ
16. Ⓐ Ⓑ Ⓒ Ⓓ
17. Ⓐ Ⓑ Ⓒ Ⓓ
18. Ⓐ Ⓑ Ⓒ Ⓓ
19. Ⓐ Ⓑ Ⓒ Ⓓ
20. Ⓐ Ⓑ Ⓒ Ⓓ
21. Ⓐ Ⓑ Ⓒ Ⓓ
22. Ⓐ Ⓑ Ⓒ Ⓓ
23. Ⓐ Ⓑ Ⓒ Ⓓ
24. Ⓐ Ⓑ Ⓒ Ⓓ
25. Ⓐ Ⓑ Ⓒ Ⓓ

English/Language Arts, Section 2

26. Ⓐ Ⓑ Ⓒ Ⓓ
27. Ⓐ Ⓑ Ⓒ Ⓓ
28. Ⓐ Ⓑ Ⓒ Ⓓ
29. Ⓐ Ⓑ Ⓒ Ⓓ
30. Ⓐ Ⓑ Ⓒ Ⓓ
31. Ⓐ Ⓑ Ⓒ Ⓓ
32. Ⓐ Ⓑ Ⓒ Ⓓ
33. Ⓐ Ⓑ Ⓒ Ⓓ
34. Ⓐ Ⓑ Ⓒ Ⓓ
35. Ⓐ Ⓑ Ⓒ Ⓓ
36. Ⓐ Ⓑ Ⓒ Ⓓ
37. Ⓐ Ⓑ Ⓒ Ⓓ
38. Ⓐ Ⓑ Ⓒ Ⓓ
39. Ⓐ Ⓑ Ⓒ Ⓓ
40. Ⓐ Ⓑ Ⓒ Ⓓ
41. Ⓐ Ⓑ Ⓒ Ⓓ
42. Ⓐ Ⓑ Ⓒ Ⓓ
43. Ⓐ Ⓑ Ⓒ Ⓓ
44. Ⓐ Ⓑ Ⓒ Ⓓ
45. Ⓐ Ⓑ Ⓒ Ⓓ
46. Ⓐ Ⓑ Ⓒ Ⓓ
47. Ⓐ Ⓑ Ⓒ Ⓓ
48. Ⓐ Ⓑ Ⓒ Ⓓ
49. Ⓐ Ⓑ Ⓒ Ⓓ
50. Ⓐ Ⓑ Ⓒ Ⓓ

CUT HERE